The Little Book
of
Longing and Despair

Sumanta Dhar

Woven Words Publishers OPC Private Limited

Registered Office: Vill: Raipur, P.O: Raipur Paschimbar, Dist: Purba Midnapore, Pin: 721401, West Bengal, India.
Branch Office(Operational): 8-1-346/19/A/1, Brindavan Colony, Tolichowki, Hyderabad-500008

www.wovenwordspublishers.com
Email: publish@wovenwordspublishers.com
First published by Woven Words Publishers OPC Pvt. Ltd., 2019

POETRY

IMPRINT: WOVEN WORDS FIRE

ISBN 13: 978-93-88762-31-1
ISBN 10: 93-88762-31-2
MRP: 300 INR

This book is a work of fiction. All names, characters, places, addresses and incidents are fictitious and product of the author's imagination. Any resemblance with any events, locales, persons-living or dead, is purely coincidental.

The author asserts the moral right to be identified as the author of this work.

Printed and bound in India by Woven Words Publishers.

If I ever have nurtured any literary ambition, it always was, writing anything, in the form of prose. Bringing out a book on poetry was never in my remotest possible aspiration.

Long ago in few notebooks mostly meant for a privately occupied prose related, yet unpublished write ups, there had been a few unplanned yet perhaps seemingly spontaneous and sketchy scribbling which felt like poetry if not in form but in spirit and vice versa: on rereading them again and again.

Along with them I have added a few more and put them in a book form: The Little Book of Longing and Despair-the title you may be holding now.

I am still not sure if these produces are yet fully grown and apt enough for a connoisseur's tastes. Therefore, if you find them inedible please do not hesitate to stow them away into the bin. I will know. Nevertheless, I won't assure you falsely of cleaning your trash cans but next time I will try to harvest more ripened variants to welcome you. Or else otherwise I would know backwater tongue had been faithful and I had been ushered in.

Thank you.

CONTENTS

For Maa and Baba

Cats on the wall

The fence; which is a lime painted wall, upon that
Often stretch their legs; a few cats
And slip into deep busy slumber and yawn
Ere they are alarmed when
Smell of fishbone, broken
Remains of the fish skull
The inedible edibles, together
Fly past them; good news
Onto the street; stall
And they creating a bow of the spine
Hold for a moment on the toes
Ere diving; snapping and rending
The lazy, idle and useless time
Now more so with the
Gnawing and licking
On the left over; picking
On the right and the left

Null days

As the orchestra of buzzing flies plays on
In a jiffy
The throat caught, shrieking
Between hook of fingers
With urgent reflex soon pressed down
On the surface that's
Dark brown, with crimson streaks; flat
A chomped of portion of
A tree trunk; dwarfish
Amidst, the body shakes, the claws pedal in air
Resistance, futile
In assured violation
The always abhorring eyes that are flaring out, still
Would soon be numb
With a deft, infallible stroke of the cleaver
And that will be the end of all
All the shrill music and croaking
And the fleeting, unimportant
Ecological atrocity, until before
Someone says repeat; repeat again

Lizards

My granny on her way back home
After keeping with her rendezvous
At the religious congregation of Vaishnavites
She would carry lozenges, round and white like those of lizard
eggs
In a small paper sack; a newspaper artifact
And I would turn angry if she would forget about it
It used to be unspoken promises at
Both our ends
Afterwards the memory of lizard
Or rather the fear of it
Or the blood itching feel of disgust
Would be there at, in the corner of
One of those lines of lavatories at my aunt's house
Underneath the shade of trees
Whose names I don't recall anymore
Or I never knew.
Later I had to topple once
A chess board
Between a half-finished game
At a friend's house, evident with
Those hairy, fiercely quivering legs of
An enormous spider, jutting out from the mouth
The glazed eyed reptile
Scampering past the green-lime painted wall
Almost grazing my half sleeve shirt
And then those fair looking breed
Gorging on banana and mango slices
In my animal loving teacher's house
Unbelievable, in the summer nights

And then these days our apartment is inundated
Filled with geckos, the infants, juveniles and the adults
I get to know it's everywhere
In the community meeting

Do egg shells frighten them? Pesticides?
Suggestions pour in and the best of all
Was to thrash and thrash them at sight
With a broom stick, until it's over; the fight

Killing a cat fish

The cat fish if you know them
Is not easy to catch and hold
It's pretty precarious until
You could have beaten it down cold; but
The fishmonger lad is adroit and bold
In waylaying his costly fare, with patience
Into a polythene pack, the head first; that's dangerous
The tail tailing the smothered cranium sways; tempestuous
Outside the bag, before coming to rest, always one last jerk
As blood fills in the translucent head scarf
Concluding the fleeting asphyxiation in all possible swiftness
And then the wooden mace smite
And truncate the redundant inflexible jaws rested
On the fish knife; large shining and bright
The whiskers and fins are clean shaved,
Gill pulled out with thumb
And the body coaxed into the blade
Once twice or thrice with aplomb
Depending on what length it was
And on your possible instructions
That you have been dictating
All the while, all these minutes.

My mother's fear

Very near to my mother's house
When she was still a girl,
Deep in the night
She would wake up frightened; alone;
Or sometimes with my aunts
As the terrific cries of the pigs would
Float and fill in her ears
And that's how appalling the scream
Of boars listen like, when butchered she would tell
And she would always murmur this story, unfailingly
On the way back to our house
As if the dreaded sound clung to her ears still
And how astonishing I too wished to
Press my ears hard
As we approached the railway ticket counter
That faced the abattoir
As if the sound still hangs on, to petrify me, us
Even in the broad glaring daylight
And I keep a vigil on my mother's countenance

Meat shop

If you happen to pass by a meat shop
Where you get freshly cut mutton
Which was a goat a while before; stop

As a testimony of their identity
A passport to a Hindu kitchen; on the shop floor
There are severed goat heads, shut eyed, placid

Above which are soon to be vanished
The gatekeepers; the hanging carcasses
Open and cut, open and cut

Glittering under the flashing bulb
As if it was an exhibition
Of permanent retribution

Contraband

"Want to buy one Midnapore Hilsha?"
Stealthily whispers the fishmonger bloke
I raise my eyes from the red cemented platform; where
different genera
Are kept in separate clumps, to meet his with utmost curiosity

He repeats: "Want to buy one Midnapore Hilsha?"
No Hilsha on sight, I say awkwardly that I didn't get him;
even this time
And by this time with a thief's wary eye around
He brings out something which looks like a fermented flat
dough

And then still with one thief's eye around
He murmurs and I too see the dough has a head and neck
And paws and legs; and I get him now and what he was
telling me
That the dough with face and limb is indeed a living creature;
a turtle

I don't ask him and don't know yet the genesis of the code or
the connotation
But I felt how contagious the fishmonger's gaze is
As now mine too is a thief's eye
As I read it in his now steadily brightening eyes

The flying ants

When in the dark a lamp is lit up,
Often in the halo of the illumination,
One can see the darkness playing hide and seek,

Whereas the strong flame at the centre,
Glows intensely,
And it slays the darkness

And also some insects,
Who prance upon the sharp light,
To pronounce, they are giving up
Slowly; their lives.
And then they drop dead and get mingled,
With the piercing darkness

Dusk by the sea shore

Underneath our feet; on the dunes
There are tiny unlit doors; ajar
And we watch the petite crabs
Streams of vermillion, weightless creatures
Scurry past circling our limbs, the legs of the plastic chairs
To and fro; busy
Playing hide and seek; doing chores
Disappearing into or peering up
From one window then the other
Through the tunnels of sand capillaries
Underneath our feet; on the dunes

In one of those shacks
Those line the shore; here we are enjoying
A sunset that has left lovely striations on the sky
With sand grain laden wet toes and heels and knees
And then we hark and beckon the man
"Crabs! We want to have crabs."
Grinning, the man retreats into
The hut that silhouettes the bamboo pillared space
Dotted with clusters of plastic chairs and tables
In one of such arrangements we are now occupying
He reemerges with his wares
Crabs scuttling; on a large bowl
We need to choose and mark
We point; as we scrutinize
The one with the fleshy claws
The one with the eggs; the female folks
No the smaller ones; soft meat
Argument and laughter a bit
And there are fowls too

The man tries to woo
"Would you come inside and have a peek?"
The man again speaks!

We walk through; following him
The light around is mostly dim
And as we climb the clay stairs into the hut
In the engulfing darkness
Ours eyes walk into the smoldering hearth
On which a cauldron has the thrashed claws, onion shells
Being tossed over by the woman
And they are glowing and glowing and glowing
Underneath our aching eyes

The Half-Slain Soldier

Often, I pretend
To put up a fight
With my future
Like a shadow
It teases me
By remaining elusive
Nevertheless, just yesterday
When I cared to spare a moment
In front of our humble mirror
I saw my jaded face
Trying to jerk up a smile
But in vein
Like a soldier
Half slain

Beside Railway Tracks

Across the railway tracks
There are shabby houses
Mortars peeling off from the walls Somewhere an
unimaginative paint
Adores the window grating
Somewhere from in every morning
Emanates the sound of a noisy radio
Budging ultimately in the
Feeble slapping strokes
Of the octogenarian
The radio, which his in-laws
May have presented him
Almost half a century ago
From the gate-less entrance
At the ground floor
Where the stairs begin
Out of the bleak darkness
Comes out a mother
Thin, week, gaudily dressed
Along with her kids
One clinging to her shoulder
Barely one year
And a daughter and son
Dressed in school uniform
They disappear at the turn of the street
A few urchins
Clad in dust and shorts
Play with a semi-defunct cycle tire
Rolling it with a short bamboo stick

They have no obligation with time
Amidst all
The shabby, mortar-less houses
Gasp like a nagging geriatrics

An appointment

Often life stops at me
As if to gasp a few more ounce of air
Looking as if lost
It gazes with its much-endured eyes
Resembling the look of a scared street dog
Seeking a pail of water and refuge.
There is no escapade
We have reduced our life to that stage.
And so the street dog barking all of a sudden,
Reminds us we are alive.

Counting the Star

When the dusk sets in
And the street lamps shimmer
The tiny shop at the corner of the lane
Starts serving fried eggplants and other oil fries
People start thronging inside buses
The cinema halls get filled up
Then on the street the kids and women
Who share and boast the pavements
Across my city
May stare at the sky
Not getting caught up
In bemusement
Because, because
They know to count the stars.

Nation Saviours

A few people
Standing there
Are gossiping
On the fate of their nation
While the nation
Smiles; her lips
Laden with melancholia
That of an uncared mother.

Post marriage adieu to a Bengali Girl
(From a daguerreotype photo)

The yellow taxi
Pulls on slowly
Near the flower bedecked gate
The smell of one-night stale petals
The faded hue of blooms
Tries to appeal the onlooker
One last time
May be.
A face appears above
From the balcony
And swiftly disappears
A commotion ensues
A slight din
Prominent in the silence
Of winter dawn
The pale orange glow
Had just started
Smearing the eastern sky
There come from within
Ululation and shrill cry
Of women folks
Resonate near the stair case
The bride in a red sari
The vermillion on her forehead
Is bright as sunlight of a summer day
Her eyes swollen
Welling up more tears
She clings from one shoulder to another

Sometimes her mother
And then to her brother
She tries to hide her crying face
Somewhere.

The embarrassed groom,
Tries to put up a pensive face,
Laced with a hint of impatience
They board the taxi, aided.
A couple of relatives from both sides pack in too
And the roar of the taxi engine is drowned
In the surging of now more strident pitch
That of weeping and shower of ululation
The taxi recedes away

A cautionary note

Shall you live well,
Then never try to understand life,
Said somebody teacher-like,
And all students in unison said,
Well, we will follow that,
Rather we will not indulge into,
All things which are
Redundant to our heart.

Terror of the blank page

I wish one day
I fill up all the pages
Churn out all the thoughts
From the maze of my mind
My mind, which is no longer
A straight road,
Keeps curving with its
All stubbornness
And all the meaningless words
With their impotency
Ravish the blank pages

The promise

How many days?
I do not know,
One will allow me
Just to scribble.
And I do not know how!
How will I manage to,
Tell you a story
Long promised.

A few faceless names

A few nameless faces, a few faceless names
Walk through lane after lane
They vanish at one turn of the street
And again get disgorged into another
They shout in rhythm
They talk on freedom

Humming noise of engines
Emancipates from the halted cars
In the prosaic traffic signal
Gets mingled with the chorus
Tired dejected faces hang on
The windows of cars and buses

The passerby doesn't pay any heed
If any, not more than a scornful glance
They keep on shouting
They demand for progress
Amidst lot many deaf ears
Their act resembles a crude ventriloquism

The cavalcade moves on
Piercing through lane to lane
They seek progress
They talk freedom
Quite oblivious, somewhere
Somewhere in the time warp,
Progress has also progressed,
A myriad light years,

Much ahead of them
And they can never progress
Except from lane to lane.
Though, they keep walking

They keep shouting
A too many faceless names, a too many nameless faces.

An amateur's ode to sound

I am not drawn by the sight
But the rustle and roar of it
As if it is chained and pained.
Or it is just how it talks when it meets the plain?
With the music in my ear,
I walk along to behold the yet unseen,
I feel like someone who doesn't see light
Sound is his world
And an epiphany dawns upon me that
We are all born blind
And how pally we were
Before light saw us
When quite impossibly
Sound and light were same.

A bit of wisdom

It's easy to walk
In the dark; one
Just needs to carry a lantern
Vaulted within
That brightens up
And saves the limbs
From the strewn shards of glass
That the darkness
Might often split into
And prick the soul

A little boy's revenge

The little boy, all of ten or less
Has something in his pockets
He touches them from time to time
The picked-up stones and pebbles
From the roadside dust and grime
And then he saunters up and down
The nooks and alleyways of the neighborhood
And keeps an eye around
To avenge his father's lashes on him
Endless ritual of preying on street dogs and feline

What I see from the terrace

There are houses too many, hugging each other
Often clubbed and clogged
Stones, cement and sand
And uneven and often disemboweled bitumen loops, around;

The discs that drink waves and excrete
In our drawing rooms; waste that bathes us
And the waste that we don't clean
Because we don't know

Protruding out from the middleclass rooftops are
Ample raised scaly, geometric palms of demons
And the sweat drops from them keep us on perpetual flood
We swim and drown

The clamped grave organs of the cooling devices;
And braids of iron bars; the skeletons
The skeletons on which
The flesh of mortars would grow

And they are too many
Just too many of them
Here and there; filling
Up the larynx; nostrils of the pinned down helpless giant

And in summer, even when the neon lights slog
It's still unbearable as each one of us
Spew heat venom on each other
Living or lifeless akin in the game

A genuine hoax

There is a little black van parked
At the three-point intersection
On a now deserted streetscape
As now it's time for the phantoms
The clock having already chimed a dozen
Under a supremely starry and moonlit night

But there are two men with jute sacks
Patrolling down the street; determination on their faces

It's an innocuous abduction scheme
Which nobody would report
That of picking up stray canines
And take them to non-proliferation pogrom
That we knew; until a decade later almost
We were told one fine morning
That we had dog meat
On our very plate

Waiting for the rain

The grey sad sky loomed large overhead
Since long and rain was still on the loose
And we longed that the sky
Should soon surrender to gravity
Freefall
And then there was rain
The awaited moment of the
Cauldron of the heaven
Turned upside down
Pouring on the soil
That's close to our heart
And then the air filled with
Ecstasy and happiness of a child
Bathing on her own

Slow evening

How earnestly I long for an evening
The one in which I wouldn't need to
Attend to nobody's beckoning

The monstrosity of the attention seeking cell-phone
I long, would be tamed for some time; but not
That time which can be gulped in few swigs

A kind of that evening; a kind of that evening
That my father had, when I was his child
A slow, tempered evening with no rush

A kind of that evening; where we may have even
A communal television watch or may be a late-night play
In the radio; followed by the closure remarks of the anchor
And why not even such evening of an unannounced arrival
Of a guest, an aunt or a distant relative to ask how we were
And me darting down to the local sweet shop to bring in
delicacies

And even I may take a train down to the station
Where the Kali temple is with my folks
And run amok in the temple courtyard, brimming with joy;
may be just like when I was a boy

Or why not just sit down on the steps of the Ganges
Flowing abreast the ancient shrine and watch lazily the setting
sun
The unhurried gliding of a fisherman's canoe

And a kerosene-stove in slow blaze glimpsing through the
little canopy of a shade
And the scent of burnt onion, garlic wafting into the air
Or may be an evening as such when I could take a double-
decker

Having a seat by the window and with the skyscrapers in sight
At the Esplanade I could alight
And walk up to the Ochterloney Monument and be amused
at its height

Or a slow evening in my house, lonely, my father away into
work
And my mother with the conch shell near the tiny cemented
rostrum
From which grew the basil plant; in our courtyard

And the lit-up lamp, incense sticks; their smokes together
clubbed
Floating and going up and up before mingling with the color
of the evening
And then far back when the evening would fall back in the
lap of impregnable darkness

Like a baby of the chirping crickets in thickets of canna lily
Rampaging little bats overhead, fireflies diving around the
cocklebur plants
And then I could say, I had my evening; I have my evening;
now

Sprint

There are two trains; green painted
With empty seats; none of my friends there
Both are running parallel

Connected by an over bridge and
Also carried by the locomotives
The bridge too is running

And there are flower brackets
Those ensnare the bridge
The trains; the window grilles, the cylindrical buffers

The unmanned driver cabins has a orange glow
That of a bedroom lamp
As if it was time to go to sleep

And the trains are running
As also the over bridge
In this magical hour

Modern conjuring

A suitcase by his side,
Presumably a salesman
Standing alone in an empty
And barren landscape
Waiting for a bus
Which may or may not come
The man walks up to
Another barren space
Unties his shoe laces
And sits down on air
And he floats
Which he doesn't acknowledge and
The barren space walks into him
And he performs a few acrobatic stunts
As if he was a pro
And then a little later
There is rain of which

No water comes down and none is drenched
The salesman slightly perturbed now
Draws them down: on his own
And it becomes a city; a part is village
And then there is a bit of rain from the painted clouds
And there are claps and hoots
There are then claps and hoots

A plausible noir story

There is little house
Yellow walled and red tiled
Around which ran a pink colored wooden barricade
Behind the house is a small railway station

And on the solitary platform
There is a tiny teashop besides the tiny bookstore
And a single coach engine
Is resting on the rail

A man emerges out of the little house
Looks back where on the doorstep
A woman waves her hand
He waves back, grins

Shortly he walks through the backside lane
And enters the teashop after buying
The day's newspaper from the bookstore,
Rolled under his sleeve

With a cup of tea he sits on a chair
With a window in front that oversees the little house
The whistle of the departing train drowns the screeching
sound of the tires
Of the car approaching the quarter

Visibility lost, he pays attention to the sounds now
That of heavy crushing notes emanating from the pebbled
pathway
Unlocking and locking of the door
And peals of laughter

He tosses couple of coins at the counter
Now the train is slowly leaving the platform
He walks back, retracing his path
Back to the house

Nocturnal pray

Late in the night
A rattling sound
That of a motorbike engine
Ricocheted through the empty lane
Lingering a light year of time
In such night mothers must be at work
I think; the moon is slightly shrunk too
Turning her face away; cringing
Unwilling to be burdened anymore
With unpleasant memories; I too with
The unnerving clamor in my ear
Yearn for clean asphalt next morning
With no tinge of crimson
And I attempt to get back to my sleep

A tale from an improbable vision

We are forced to slow down
Our car; and we can see ourselves
Converging into vast swathes of automobiles,
Still grazing; like foam
On a washroom floor
Shortly we also fit in, getting added
Like a freshly generated bubble
Also, the other cars side by side
And we coalesce; not bursting

On this high-speed corridor
Impossibility impending, at each other we stare
Grimacing; jaws drooping, exasperated
As if it was a thwarted intromission after a long foreplay
Because a baby crying in the other room
Or an unexpected arrival of guest

And through the opening of the roofs
Of the convertibles there are bodies, plant like
Sprouting out for getting to know
What lies at the end of this gliding ripple of cars?

Ahead only a man with bicycle, mimicking a snail's motion
Has caused this catastrophe; trimming down our acceleration

News this unbelievable travels to us in no time
And we start honking, yelling and calling names
Roll our sleeves, flip the collars up and march
To get the man who has robbed our speed; baying for blood

We trickle through the narrow mazes
Between the vehicles with vehemence, anger
Alike pent up hot lava of a volcano turned active
Suddenly through an unwarranted tectonic shift
But then no sooner each one of us could have walked a few
steps
Our legs turned wobbly and the cars throbbed

And to our sheer dismay we saw the corridor of speed
beginning to tilt downward
As if it was broken in the middle like a piece of wafer then!
But how!
And with supreme awe we observe ourselves having to trundle
along the slope and the cars too
And someone with a genuinely capable pitch screams
"Clutch on! Hold on! He is pushing us back with his
slowness."

And I felt now the lava freezing inside; the bicycle man,
outraging, robbing us off our
Carefully nurtured, fascinatingly adored and lusted speed
with his stupid slowness
And I recall a scene from childhood that of me pricking
On the retreating bubbles of foam in the washroom or
somewhere else

The new kid on the block

There is no war anymore
Me and you in bliss and
Here I am
With you all
Together again

Sipping slowly
From the long infinite glass
Of facts

And often I
With you all
Get woozy and faint
And do a little fight

Still yet
We hug the glass; twirl
And kiss it; also often
Snort from the pit of it

Facts here they come
In sneezes, in blows and blizzards
And we press our hankies hard on the nose
Or cower under our folded elbows

And then we are there
At a doctor's place
With tingling eyes, clogged ears

Our teeth are soft like gels
And gums do bleed

So, we have our calcium pills

Here is actually the new dope
That you and I take
From the infinite long glass
The mud and debris of facts

We feel tipsy
In delirium always
As the glass we thought of is
Indeed, the new syringe with new coke
And in hand with it
We feel high and light

Therefore, with no war anymore
You and I in bliss
You and I in bliss

Ribbon of time

And then I see
Someone approaching me
And then another one
And then more and more of them; all together
Slowly and also fast anyhow they come to slaughter
Whose child I am; the time
And a large scissor cuts it like a ribbon
In useless pieces and I scramble through
To put them together
As I see them strewn all over;
Here and there; here and there

Acknowledgements

My heartfelt gratitude to the Remington type-writer, overhead bookcase, stacks of newspapers, at my English teacher Anil Mukherjee's house and most to him for helping me fall in love with seeing, thinking, reading and writing on my own, prodding whenever I failed to remain tenacious, reiterating the almost sent-to-oblivion significance of human values.

Abundant love for Maharshi, our four year old child for letting me write, giving up his share of my little time, wherein I could have been his horse, reading pal or playmate.

Maitreyee, my wife, who with only a little grudge allowed me to pursue an almost *luftmensch* approach towards life given today's set protocols, kept the family knitted, understood without display, took the toil of mundane familial responsibilities: to her my deepest appreciation and adoration.

Notes

www.ingramcontent.com/pod-product-compliance
Lightning Source LLC
Chambersburg PA
CBHW030410160726
47992CB00007B/3054